W9-ALM-025

AMERICAN HOLIDAYS

★ ★

Passover

Tamar Lupo

j296.437
LUP

Weigl Publishers Inc.

Published by Weigl Publishers Inc.
350 5th Avenue, Suite 3304, PMB 6G
New York, NY 10118-0069
Web site: www.weigl.com

Copyright © 2007 WEIGL PUBLISHERS INC.
All rights reserved.   No part of this publication may be reproduced,
stored in a retrieval system, or transmitted in any form or by any means,
electronic, mechanical, photocopying, recording, or otherwise, without
the prior written permission of the publisher.

Library of Congress Cataloging-in-Publication Data

TamLupo, Tamar.
  Passover / Tamar Lupo.
       p. cm.
  Includes index.
  ISBN 1-59036-462-7 (hard cover : alk. paper) -- ISBN 1-59036-465-1 (soft cover : alk. paper)
  1. Passover--Juvenile literature. I. Title.
  BM695.P3L87 2007
  296.4'37--dc22
                                        2006016149

Printed in the United States of America
1 2 3 4 5 6 7 8 9 0 10 09 08 07 06

Editor Heather C. Hudak
Design and Layout Terry Paulhus

Cover A Rabbi serves food at
the seder meal during Passover.

All of the Internet URLs given in the book were valid at the time of publication. However, due to the dynamic nature of the Internet, some addresses may have changed, or sites may have ceased to exist since publication. While the author and publisher regret any inconvenience this may cause readers, no responsibility for any such changes can be accepted by either the author or the publisher.

Every reasonable effort has been made to trace ownership and to obtain permission to reprint copyright material. The publishers would be pleased to have any errors or omissions brought to their attention so that they may be corrected in subsequent printings.

Contents

Introduction

★ ★

Passover is one of the most important Jewish holidays.

Passover is a holiday celebrated on the 15th day of the **Hebrew** month' of *Nisan*. It is celebrated for eight days. Passover is one of the most important **Jewish** holidays and remembers how the Hebrews left Egypt and were freed from slavery.

For many years, Jewish people around the world have celebrated Passover with a feast called a *seder*, which means "order." The order of the meal and the stories that are told at the seder are very important. Families read a book called the *Haggadah* at the seder. It tells them in what order the meal should be eaten.

DiD YOU KNOW?

The first Haggadah was printed in 1770, in London, England.

Jewish families pray together before starting the seder dinner during the Passover festival.

The History of Passover

★ ★

Moses asked the Pharaoh to free the slaves.

I n Ancient Egypt, the Pharaoh, or ruler, had Hebrew slaves. A young prince named Moses hated to see the slaves treated so badly.

Moses asked the Pharaoh to free the slaves. The Pharaoh refused, and so ten **plagues** were sent to Egypt. The tenth plague was the death of all first-born sons. To save the children, Jewish people believe God told Moses to have each Hebrew family make a mark on their doors with the blood of a lamb so that the Angel of Death would "pass over" them.

The Pharaoh called Moses and told him to take his people out of Egypt. The Hebrews ran into the desert with only a few animals and dough that did not have time to rise for bread.

DID YOU KNOW?

The Pharaoh's name was Ramses the Second, and he lived more than 3,000 years ago.

However, the Hebrews were not safe. The Pharaoh chased after them. Jewish people believe that a **miracle** happened when the Hebrews reached the Red Sea. The sea parted in two so that the Hebrews could walk across safely. After the Hebrews finished crossing, the sea closed, stopping the Pharoah's soldiers from following them.

One of the ten plagues was a plague of frogs.

The Four Questions

★ ★

At the seder, the youngest child must answer four questions.

To pass on the traditions and stories of the holiday, parents involve children in the Passover meal. During the seder, children are asked four questions by an adult. The youngest child at the table must answer the four questions. These questions help children to understand why some foods, such as the hard cracker called the matzoh, are only eaten at the Passover meal. The four questions are also put in song, and the whole family sings the questions and answers.

DID YOU KNOW?

The woman of the house begins the seder by saying a blessing over the Passover candles.

A traditional seder plate has six foods that symbolize the different parts of the Passover story.

8

Horseradish root is mixed with beets, vinegar, and sugar to make Passover horseradish.

Passover Traditions

★ ★

The Passover meal includes prayers and songs.

Passover is a joyful, eight-day holiday and has many wonderful traditions throughout the world. The Passover meal has a set order that includes prayers and songs. Children ask many questions and sing songs.

The meal is made up of traditional foods, such as chicken soup with matzoh balls, fruits, vegetables, and salads. There is matzoh brei, made of matzoh, cinnamon, and egg. There are also lamb dishes and cakes made of matzoh and honey.

★ ★ ★ ★ ★ ★ ★ ★

Children play a very important part in the Passover meal.

The Cup of Elijah

The cup of Elijah is put out to invite Elijah the **Prophet** to join in the seder. Elijah watched over the Hebrew community in hard times.

During the seder, Jewish people do not drink from the cup of Elijah because it is reserved for the prophet.

Passover in the Past

★ ★

At Passover, people removed bread and yeast from their homes.

For thousands of years, the most important parts of Passover were the removing of bread and yeast from the house, and having a large meal with family and friends. It was also a great *mitzvah*, or good deed, to invite people who had no family of their own, or strangers who had little food, to join in the meal. Their tables would be covered in fresh fish, wheat cakes, honey, and wine.

★ ★ ★ ★ ★ ★ ★ ★ ★
Some people celebrate Passover at the remains of the old Hebrew temple in Jerusalem.

In ancient times, each person went to the temple in Jerusalem to pray and celebrate as one large family. When Jewish people came to the United States, each group built their own smaller synagogues and gathered there to pray. A synagogue is a place of worship for Jews. The people lived very close to their synagogues because, during the holiday, they were not allowed to drive or even ride a bike. People would walk together to synagogue instead.

DID YOU KNOW?

In ancient times, people would bring a lamb to the great temple in Jerusalem as a spring offering, or gift.

In 1897, a synogogue was built near Central Park in New York City for the first Jewish congregation founded in the United States.

Passover Today

★ ★

People go to the synagogue to pray.

DID YOU KNOW?

In 1982, five women, including U.S. Representative Bella Abzug, celebrated what is thought to be the first women's seder in the United States.

Passover is celebrated in the United States today much as it was in the past. People remove all the bread and yeast from their home, and they spend time praying in the synagogue. After synagogue, they share the Passover meal with family and friends. Today, they also get involved in their communities and try to bring people of all faiths together through music, lectures, and big community seders. Some synagogues put on model seders in order to help teach families how to put on seder at home.

Many North American Jews have added some special things to the Haggadah. They write about freedom in the United States, and they feel it is a good idea to help people who are not enjoying freedom and equality.

Synagogues hold special services during Passover.

Americans Celebrate

Passover is celebrated across the United States. This map shows a few events that take place each year, as well as a special event that broke a world record one year.

In Boston, MIT **Hillel** sponsors a seder on each of the first two nights of this eight-day holiday. Hillel also sponsors programs for Jewish and non-Jewish students to learn more about the holiday and its practices and traditions.

The National Jewish Outreach Program, based in New York, has introduced "Passover Across America." This program provides seders for people who otherwise could not attend one. Today, this seder takes place in 20 locations across the United States.

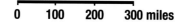

0   100   200   300 miles

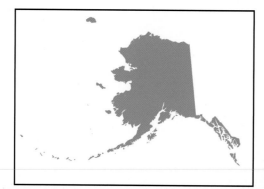

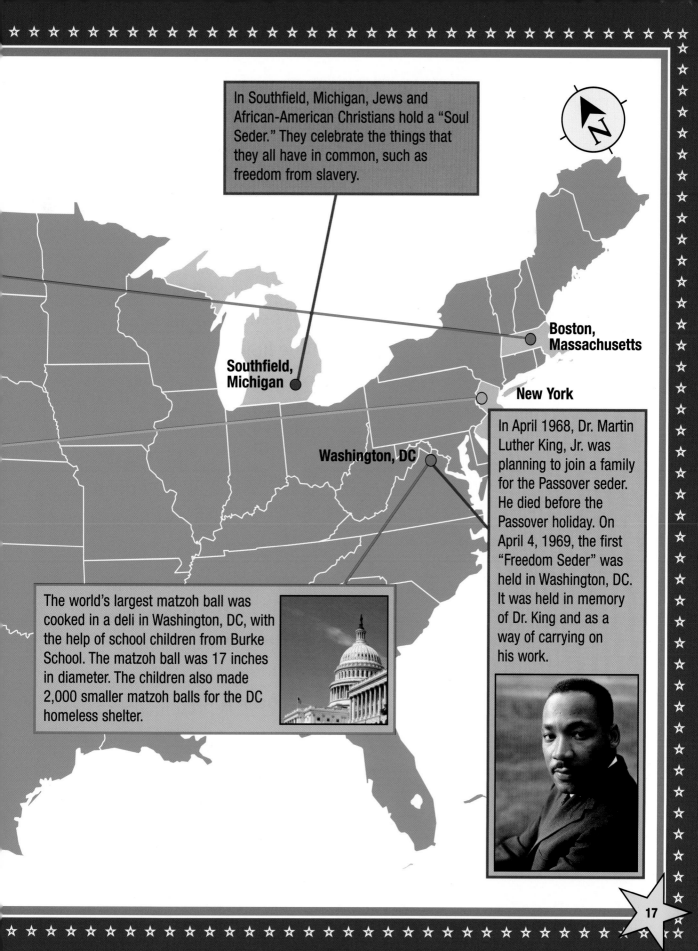

In Southfield, Michigan, Jews and African-American Christians hold a "Soul Seder." They celebrate the things that they all have in common, such as freedom from slavery.

Boston, Massachusetts

Southfield, Michigan

New York

Washington, DC

In April 1968, Dr. Martin Luther King, Jr. was planning to join a family for the Passover seder. He died before the Passover holiday. On April 4, 1969, the first "Freedom Seder" was held in Washington, DC. It was held in memory of Dr. King and as a way of carrying on his work.

The world's largest matzoh ball was cooked in a deli in Washington, DC, with the help of school children from Burke School. The matzoh ball was 17 inches in diameter. The children also made 2,000 smaller matzoh balls for the DC homeless shelter.

Holiday Symbols

Passover has many different symbols. Here are two of the best-known Passover symbols in America.

Matzoh

Matzoh is made of flour and water and baked in a very hot oven. When it is done baking, it has little holes poked into it to allow steam out. A special piece of matzoh, called the *afikomen*, is hidden in the house during the seder, and the children make a game of finding it. It can then be eaten as a dessert at the end of the meal. Usually, the child that finds the hidden afikomen in the house is presented with a special gift.

★ ★ ★ ★ ★ ★ ★ ★ ★

The afikomen is wrapped in a napkin, or a specially decorated afikoman bag.

Seder Plate

There are six spaces on the seder plate for foods that help tell the story of Passover. Horseradish often represents *maror,* or bitter herbs. It is a symbol of the bitter years of slavery in Egypt. Lettuce is often used to represent the bitter vegetable, or *chazaret.* This symbolizes the bitter lives of the slaves. *Charoset* is made from apples, nuts, spices, and wine. It is a symbol of the cement Jewish slaves used to build Egyptian cities.

Karpas, or vegetable, represents the coming of spring and new things. It is usually dipped into salt water that represents the tears shed in Egypt by the slaves. *Zeroa,* or shank bone, symbolizes the lamb offered to God at Passover. *Beitzah,* or egg, is a symbol of the hard heart of the Pharaoh and the hard times Jewish slaves survived. It also symbolizes spring.

Further Research

Many books and websites explain the history and traditions of Passover. These resources can help you learn more.

Websites

To learn about Passover, visit:

www.kidsdomain.com/holiday/passover

www.chadiscrafts.com/fun

Books

Barbara Rush and Cherie Karo Schwartz. *The Kids Catalog of Passover: A Worldwide Celebration of Stories, Songs, Customs, Crafts, Food and Fun.* New York: Jewish Publication Society of America, 2000.

Judyth Saypol Groner. *All About Passover.* Kar-Ben Publishing, 2000.

Crafts and Recipes

Make a Seder Plate

Use a strong paper plate. Cut out pictures of eggs, parsley, lettuce, apples, and nuts from magazines, or draw your own pictures. Glue or draw the pictures all around the inside of the plate. Paint the edge of the plate with designs.

Afikomen Bag

To make an afikomen bag, cut two pieces of colored felt about 10 inches x 12 inches. Glue three sides together, leaving the fourth side open to slip in the piece of matzoh. You can decorate the felt using markers and glitter glue.

Chicken Soup with Matzoh Balls Recipe

Ingredients

Matzoh Balls
  3 eggs beaten
  1/2 teaspoon salt
  3 tablespoons hot water
  1/2 cup matzoh meal

Chicken Soup
  1 frying chicken
  1 teaspoon salt
  1 teaspoon pepper
  1 celery stalk
  1 carrot
  1 onion
  1 piece of cauliflower
  1 turnip
  3 sprigs parsley
  1 beef shank bone
  fresh dill to garnish

1. Mix eggs, salt, and hot water with matzoh meal, and put in refrigerator for about an hour.
2. Make matzoh balls the size of a marble.
3. Drop the matzoh balls into 2 quarts of boiling water or chicken broth. Cover and cook for 20 minutes.
4. Drain the matzoh balls from the water or broth.
5. Put all the ingredients in a large pot, and cover with water.
6. Bring ingredients to a slow boil, and let simmer for 3 hours.
7. Serve with matzoh balls and dill.

Passover Quiz

What have you learned about Passover? Answer the following true or false questions. Check your answers on the following page.

1 An important part of Passover is removing yeast and bread from the house. True or false?

2 Passover lasts for eight days. True or false?

3 Matzoh is made from apples, nuts, and cinnamon. True or false?

4 The oldest child at the seder table asks the four questions. True or false?

5 There were five plagues brought down on Egypt. True or false?

Fascinating Facts

★ During Passover, the Coca-Cola bottling company of New York makes Coke that is **kosher** for Passover. Sugar is used instead of corn syrup because corn is not considered kosher for Passover.

★ In 2005, about 72 million dozen eggs were sold at U.S. supermarkets each week. During the week of Easter and the Passover seder meal, sales climbed to more than 93 million dozen eggs. This is because many families decorate eggs for Easter or have them as part of the Passover seder meal.

★ There was a sports hero from New York named Isaac Matza. He was a track and field champ in the 1950s. *Matza* is the Hebrew word for "matzoh".

Quiz Answers:
1. True
2. True
3. False. Matzoh is made from flour and water.
4. False. An adult asks the four questions.
5. False. There were ten plagues.

Glossary

★ ★ ★ ★ ★ ★ ★ ★ ★ ★ ★ ★ ★ ★ ★ ★

Haggadah: a book that organizes the rituals to take place at a seder

Hebrew: an old name for the Jewish people and their language

Hillel: a Jewish student association across North America

Jewish: relating to people who believe in God and the Old Testament and follow only its teachings

kosher: food that is prepared following laws in the Old Testament

miracle: an amazing event

plagues: disasters that Jews believe were sent by God as a punishment

prophet: a religious teacher thought to be inspired by God

Index

★ ★ ★ ★ ★ ★ ★ ★ ★ ★ ★ ★ ★ ★ ★ ★